The Painted Tombs of Swift

BY CAROLYN BROWN

CAROLYN BROWN HAS TRAVELED THE WORLD in search of the perfect subjects to photograph. Travel grants took Carolyn to all across Mexico, Lebanon, Syria, Iraq and Turkey. These locations allowed her to capture the faraway beauty of the ancient world.

At first glimpse her photographs may not reveal Carolyn's vision, but upon closer study her message becomes evident. This is the case with the Swift Meat Packing plant in Fort Worth. The decaying buildings and the land where they rested for over 100 years at first appear to be an eyesore. Carolyn's photographs reveal something deeper—a sense of mystery and beauty as nature replaces architecture and the graphic and sometimes brutal graffiti covers many surfaces.

Once again Carolyn has successfully shared what she sees through the lens of her camera. Her vision is truly a gift both for herself and for all who have the privilege of seeing the world through her eyes.

KENNETH CRAIGHEAD, DIRECTOR OF CRAIGHEAD GREEN GALLERY

The Painted Tombs of Swift

FORT WORTH STOCKYARDS 2016

In the spring of 2016 I was hired to record the Swift Meat Packing campus for preservation records. In a career spanning four decades nothing could have prepared me for the wonderment that I would find at the site. It was utterly transformed from its original purpose.

As I worked on images, I realized I was back to the beginning of my career—back in Egypt, where I began photographing ancient sites for my studies at the American University of Cairo, or in southern Mexico along the Usumacinta River to document unrestored jungle areas of Yaxchilan and Bonampak—ancient Mayan sites left to the forces of nature.

Eight abandoned dark-red brick buildings stood crumbling on a twenty-two acre area at the end of Exchange Avenue at the Fort Worth Stock Yards. Built in 1902 and deserted in 1971, these substantial buildings were the headquarters for the Swift Meat Packing Plant, important for the success of Fort Worth as a city those many years, and they had suffered the powers of wind, rain and vandalism.

Somewhere along the way, these shells became a palette for graffiti artists, and most surfaces inside and out-side were covered with brightly colored, spray-painted designs and words. Some of the imagery was artful, some was not. The empty painted shells were reminiscent of painted tombs where spirits of the dead could peacefully reside, much like the brightly painted New Kingdom tombs on the West Bank across the Nile River from Luxor Egypt.

The shifting equilibrium between nature and man was evident as the buildings collapsed and disintegrated. Luxuriant but wild green flora was triumphant and consuming—burying a grotesque past. Trees grew on rooftops that had not collapsed, parasitic vines curled freely on many surfaces, moss grew on dripping moist ceilings feeding on the frequent spring rains of North Texas. Tall grasses with sharp bristled seeds that collect on pant legs grew with abandon. A family of beautiful raptors lived on the top of one building—which probably explained the absence of rabbits or snakes on the ground.

In the summer of 2016, not long after I made these photographs, all but two of the buildings were demolished due to failure of the existing structure. One of the buildings will be restored into a landmark and made available for man again.

CAROLYN BROWN

Swift and Company Site, Fort Worth

With the fortuitous flip of a coin, Swift and Company of Chicago chose to build its Fort Worth packing plant on the south half of a 42-acre site offered by the Fort Worth Stock Yards Company. Located on a small hill overlooking Exchange Avenue to the north and North Main Street to the west, this parcel was deemed more desirable than the northern tract, soon to be the location of the Armour and Company packing plant, because of its proximity to a streetcar line and the city's downtown. The plants erected by the two companies were very similar as both required the same types of facilities for receiving, processing, and shipping of their commodities.

Work on the plants began in early 1902. Much of the Swift site had to be cleared, graded, and leveled before actual construction could begin. In less than a year, a compact complex of interconnected buildings ranging in height from one to eight stories arose on the site. The Swift and Company headquarters building was located at the northwest corner near Exchange Avenue. Most of the buildings were constructed of red-tinted brick which provided a uniform appearance. The earliest buildings were reinforced with iron columns for supporting the upper stories and the heavy equipment required in the manufacturing process. The structural system of later buildings was composed of reinforced concrete that could be articulated as a grid pattern on the exterior. Running north/south through the center of the tract were rail lines that connected the plant to distant markets. With the exception of the construction of a few new buildings and technological upgrades, the site remained relatively unchanged during the nearly seventy years the plant was in operation.

In the post-World War II era, changes in the livestock industry included a greater dependence on truck transportation rather than rail, and the de-centralization of processing facilities. Fort Worth's Armour plant closed in 1962 and the Swift plant closed in 1971. The Swift and Company headquarters building was adapted to another use, but much of the processing plant was demolished. Those buildings constructed with reinforced concrete proved to be less susceptible to the wrecking ball. They and a few ancillary buildings were left to ruin. The intervening decades and exposure to the elements, both human and natural, transformed them into ghostly remnants of an industry that once defined Fort Worth.

SUSAN KLINE, HISTORIAN

24

Index

Matias Bilbao
YELLOWCASE, LLC
Dallas, Texas

Debra Stevens
Steven Garrett
DEBRA STEVENS FRAMING
Dallas, Texas

Gilbert Mota
Vice President
COMMERCE CONSTRUCTION
CO., LP
Fort Worth, Texas

Steve Green
Scot Presley
Kenneth Craighead
CRAIGHEAD GREEN
GALLERY
Dallas, Texas

Scott Sinnett
Sales Representative
FRIESENS
Altona MB, Canada

Susan Kline
HISTORIAN
Fort Worth, Texas

Jamie Browning
Kristin Payne Atwell
ATWELL DESIGN, INC
Dallas, Texas

ISBN: 976-0-692-81038-5

Book design by Kristin Payne Atwell and Jamie Browning, Atwell Design, Inc., Dallas, Texas.

Printed in Canada.

The Painted Tombs of Swift is available for purchase in bulk. Contact Carolyn Brown at cebphoto@swbell.net.